A Call to Effective Prayer

Tom Tirivangani

A CALL TO EFFECTIVE PRAYER

Published by
Tom Tirivangani Press and Publications
200 Sanford Ave North, Hamilton, Ontario
Canada L8L5Z8

Copyright © 2025 by Tom Tirivangani
All rights reserved. All rights reserved.
No part of this publication may be reproduced, stored in a retrieval system, or transmitted in any form or by any means except in the case of a brief quotation printed in articles or reviews without prior permission in writing from the publisher

First Printing, 2025

Unless otherwise identified, Scripture quotations are taken from the New King James Version®. Copyright © 1982 by Thomas Nelson. Used by permission. All rights reserved.

Scripture quotations identified NIV are taken from the NEW INTERNATIONAL VERSION, Holy Bible, New International Version®, NIV® Copyright ©1973, 1978, 1984, 2011 by Biblica, Inc.® Used by permission. All rights reserved worldwide.

Scripture quotations identified AMPC are taken from the Amplified Bible, Classic Edition. Copyright © 1954, 1958, 1962, 1964, 1965, 1987 by The Lockman Foundation

Contents

1 A Call to Effective Prayer   1
2 Introduction   5
3 Where Do I Start   14
4 The Burden that precedes true Prayer   20
5 Impartation as a means to effective prayer   25
6 The Evidence of the power of prayer   31
7 Prayer: The Discipline That Transforms   53

1

A Call to Effective Prayer

God has called me as a prophet to the nations. In Jeremiah 1.4-5, the prophet recalls how God called him, saying, "Then the word of the Lord came to me, saying: 'Before I formed you in the womb I knew you; Before you were born I sanctified you; I ordained you a prophet to the nations'" (Jer. 1.4-5). From the beginning, I must tell you something important: a true prophet spends most of their time talking to God so that they may communicate God's message to the people they are called to serve. You cannot be a prophet unless you are an intercessor or a prayer warrior. Every true prophet is, first and foremost, a person of prayer. The prophet must be immersed in the fragrance of prayer and must continuously communicate with God. They must be a person of prayer.

Many of the prophets in the Bible carried a burden for prayer; it is this burden that moved their prophetic ministry. Prophets are not people of designer clothes, luxurious homes, or glamorous cars. They are men and women who are immersed in the mud of human failures and struggles, wrestling to serve humanity. They are those who have rolled up their sleeves to pull people and nations out of the depths of sin, human depravity and corruption. Unfortunately, the way the prophetic ministry is often portrayed and presented in the 21st century bears little resemblance to the prophetic ministry revealed in the Holy Scriptures. Prophets are called to wrestle with human depravity, sin, and carnality, and to extricate humanity from the dangers of sin. Isaiah said that the Lord told him:

> Cry aloud, spare not; Lift up your voice like a trumpet; Tell My people their transgression, And the house of Jacob their sins. Yet they seek Me daily, And delight to know My ways, As a nation that did righteousness, And did not forsake the ordinance of their God. They ask of Me the ordinances of justice; They take delight in approaching God. 'Why have we fasted, 'they say, 'and You have not seen? Why have we afflicted our souls, And You take no notice?' "In fact, in the day of your fast you find pleasure, and exploit all your laborers. Indeed you fast for strife and debate, And to strike with the fist of wickedness. You will not fast as you do this day, to make your voice heard on high (Isa. 58.1-4).

It is clear that the call of Isaiah was not business as usual. It was not a walk in the park. God meant business with humanity. God was sick and tired of human failure and sin, and He was sending someone to call it out. Habakkuk said he had a burden: "Then the LORD answered me and said: 'Write the vision and make it plain on tablets, that he may run who reads it'" (Hab. 2.2). A burden is a heavy load, a deep conviction, a desperate call to action. When God called Nehemiah, the Bible tells us that Nehemiah had a burden that made him restless; he cried for many days with fasting and prayer.

Esther heard and understood her uncle Mordecai's burden for Israel. The danger of extermination is looming, and she could not sit idly by and watch a whole nation be destroyed by the jealousy and envy of one man. She commanded, "Go, gather all the Jews who are present in Shushan, and fast for me; neither eat nor drink for three days, night or day. My maids and I will fast likewise. And so I will go to the king, which *is* against the law; and if I perish, I perish!"

(Esth. 4.16). What incredible courage and determination! Similarly, Jeremiah was deeply touched and impressed, yet the burden burned within him, and he could not keep quiet. Imprisonment could not deter him. Micaiah, the son of Imla, was put into prison by King Ahab so that he would not prophesy doom to him. And what about Elijah, who wrestled with eight hundred false prophets? He knew in his heart that the truth, though singular, is the majority in God's Kingdom. We do not merely judge the truth by the number of people speaking it; we judge the truth by its source. Jesus says, "I am the way, the truth, and the life" (John 14.6). If Jesus says it, it does not matter who is saying the opposite. The four hundred false prophets at Ahab's table disposal could not threaten the integrity of Micaiah.

This book deals with three essential aspects of effective prayer. Here, we learn that true and effective prayer is not just prayer; it is a call. A call means an outcry, a command, or that you are being summoned. As a lawyer and jurist, I know what it means when a person is being "summoned." When a summons is issued, you cannot ignore it or make an excuse. If the court issues a summons and you do not obey, a warrant for your arrest is issued. Once found, you will be arrested and committed to prison. Similarly, the call by God, summoning you to prayer is not just an ordinary prayer but a highly organized and efficient prayer that will prompt God to act on your petition.

Many prayer meetings are ineffective because there is no thorough preparation for prayer. The prayer meeting is not well thought out; it is not structured. As a result, we end up with haphazard prayer. The second struggle in effective prayer is to jumpstart the prayer itself. When it starts, it is by the grace of God that it continues, lifting your prayer to the level of persistent, consistent, and prevailing prayer. Only then can we experience prayer that yields tremendous results for the intercessor. This can only happen when we allow the Holy Spirit to pray for us and through us.

The holy spirit has a tremendous and immeasurable ability to pray and enable us to pray. I have been amazed by the work of the Holy

Spirit in prayer. I have been and continue to be utterly blown away by the way the Spirit of God works through a person, illuminating and drawing that person closer to the Almighty God. Repeatedly, I have been ushered into the presence of God by the Holy Spirit. The Holy Spirit is indeed my comforter, my counsellor and my teacher. Sometimes I wonder, how do I know that? Or how did I come to discover that? Only the Holy Spirit can enable a person to reach such heights in prayer. Only the Holy Spirit can allow a person to reach such depths in their spiritual life, and this is the third essential aspect of effective prayer. I have always yearned for a deep, abiding relationship with the Holy Spirit. When I look at myself, I see the terrible human limitations that encamp around my life. But when I lift up my eyes to the Lord, I see another depth of insight and power: the limitless ability of the Spirit of God, the Spirit of truth, the Spirit of Christ. All fear is gone; all anxiety is gone. Only the peace that the spirit of God gives remains, and it remains permanently as long as I keep trusting the Lord. There is no effective prayer without the help of the Holy Spirit. The Holy Spirit is the oasis, the epitome of real and effective prayer.

Maintaining a relationship with the Holy Spirit is the work in which the intercessor ought to get engaged in. Here, I am referring to an intimate, loving, and living relationship with the third person of the Trinity. I love it when I am in tune with the Holy Spirit. The aura of His presence shakes all forms of carnality and gives a Christian the substance and form that the divine gives. Desire to be fully baptised by the Holy Spirit and to walk in Him and with Him. This is a relationship unlike any other. Come into fellowship with the Holy Spirit. I challenge you to seek a deeper relationship with Him, and your prayer life will not be the same again.

2

Introduction

Every battle is and must be won on your knees. When one looks up to Jesus Christ while on their knees, the floodgates of heaven open, doors open, favour flows, and wonders follow. Pray because it is the key. (Tirivangani)

Prayer is the key to unlocking the blessing of God in your life. If you want to change your life, you must learn to pray. If you want to live long, you must learn to pray. If you want good health, you must pray for it. If you want to see change in your life, you must learn to pray for it. Prayer gives meaning and direction to your life. Prayer is a lethal weapon against the schemes of Satan. If there is something Satan hates, it is a believer who has learned to pray. Prayer has the power to stop demonic and satanic activity. When there is prayer, it is difficult for Satan to operate.

Jesus had a lifestyle of prayer. It was His custom to pray. He often woke up early and went to a secluded or lonely place to pray. In Luke 6.12-13, we are told that "One of those days Jesus went out to a mountainside to pray, and spent the night praying to God. When morning came, He called His disciples to Him and chose twelve of them, whom He also named apostles." The disciples of Jesus had observed Him praying many times. They had seen John teach his disciples the discipline of prayer. One day, the disciples of Jesus approached Him and said, "Lord, teach us to pray, as John also taught his disciples" (Luke 11.1). The disciples suddenly had a deep and compelling conviction about the importance of prayer. They suddenly felt a burden surge in their hearts. They knew, by the revelation of the Holy Spirit, that they needed to know how to pray. They had observed the prayer of the Pharisees, scribes, and Sadducees, but it did not impress them. It was ritual prayer, monotonous prayer, mere vain repetitions. The prayer of Jesus Christ was different. It was deep, compelling and convicting. It was prayer filled with sincerity and love.

Earlier, Jesus had said to His disciples, "And when you pray, you shall not be like the hypocrites. For they love to pray standing in the synagogues and on the corners of the streets, that they may be seen by men. Assuredly, I say to you, they have their reward. But you, when you pray, go into your room, and when you have shut your door, pray to your Father who is in the secret place; and your Father who sees in secret will reward you" (Matt. 6.5-8).

As you read this book, it is important that God gives you a burden for prayer. Pray that God will give you a burden to pray like Jesus Christ. Jesus indeed had a compelling burden. The book of Hebrews 5.7 provides a deep insight into the manner of Jesus Christ's prayer life: "Who, in the days of His flesh, when He had offered up prayers and supplications, with vehement cries and tears to Him who was able to save Him from death, and was heard because of His godly fear" (Heb. 5.7).

In Habakkuk 1.2-4, we learn about the burden that weighed heavily on the prophet: "O Lord, how long shall I cry, and You will not hear? Even cry out to You, 'Violence!' and You will not save. Why do You show me iniquity, and cause me to see trouble? For plundering and violence are before me; there is strife, and contention arises. Therefore the law is powerless, and justice never goes forth. For the wicked surround the righteous; therefore perverse judgment proceeds." To pray effectively, one needs a burden. As you prepare to enter into a time of prayer, you must ensure that God has given you a burden. It is the burden that compels you to pray. Prayer is talking to God—talking to the One who has the power to change your circumstances. God loves to hear the prayers of His children. Every morning, He waits to hear what His children will say to Him. A break in prayer is a break in communion with God. As Psalms 34.15 tells us, "The eyes of the Lord are on the righteous, And His ears are open to their cry."

We are also told in Matthew 7.7-8: "Ask, and it will be given to you; seek, and you will find; knock, and it will be opened to you. For everyone who asks receives, and he who seeks finds, and to him who knocks it will be opened."

In Numbers 23.19, the Word of God says, "God is not a man, that He should lie, Nor a son of man, that He should repent. Has He said, and will He not do? Or has He spoken, and will He not make it good?".

God is faithful and dependable. When God makes a promise, be sure He will honour His word. The word of the Lord says that God has made Himself a slave to His word. He watches over His word to perform it. In Isaiah 55.11, we read, "So shall My word be that goes forth from My mouth; It shall not return to Me void, But it shall accomplish what I please, And it shall prosper in the thing for which I sent it."

But why are some of our prayers not answered? You have prayed and prayed, yet you have not received an answer. What is the problem? I can tell you without a shadow of a doubt that God is not the problem. But you say, "I have asked, and God has not answered." Why is it like that if God is so keen to answer my prayer? Many people take prayer as a ritual. Many do not take prayer seriously; they just pray anyhow. Effective and productive prayer requires serious preparation and planning. You cannot simply jump into prayer and expect God to answer. A lot of people pray, but they do so out of obligation, and that is why their prayers are not answered. They pray randomly, lacking wisdom and insight. The Word of God gives us insight and understanding. It is important to know that your zeal for prayer must be according to knowledge. Effective prayer must be based on knowledge of the Word of God and must also be inspired by the Holy Spirit.

Therefore, careful thought and planning are required if your prayer is to be effective.

In Luke 14.28-32, Jesus teaches: "For which of you, intending to build a tower, does not sit down first and count the cost, whether he has enough to finish it—lest, after he has laid the foundation and is not able to finish, all who see it begin to mock him, saying, 'This man began to build and was not able to finish'? Or what king, going to make war against another king, does not sit down first and consider whether he is able with ten thousand to meet him who comes against him with twenty thousand? Or else, while the other is still a great way off, he sends a delegation and asks conditions of peace."

As believers and disciples of Jesus Christ, we can never negotiate with Satan or those in the satanic kingdom. However, the direction of our battle against Satan must be well thought out. The aim of this book is to teach you how to offer effective and powerful prayer that guarantees you victory over Satan every time you pray. Satan is a master deceiver. To defeat Satan, you must climb to a higher spiritual realm. This is precisely what Jesus Christ did in the famous story of His temptation in the wilderness recorded in Matthew 4. The enemy often tempts us through our physical needs. In this story, Jesus Christ was exhausted and hungry after a long 40 days of prayer and fasting.

This was real fasting and real prayer. The tempter came to Him and said, "'If You are the Son of God, command that these stones become bread.' But He answered and said, 'It is written, "Man shall not live by bread alone, but by every word that proceeds from the mouth of God"'" (Matt. 4.3-4).

Jesus did not fight back against the enemy at the same level he was being tempted. The enemy was operating in the flesh, but Jesus rose into the spirit. He fought the devil from a spiritual point of view, causing the temptation to suddenly fall apart. Satan tried again and failed a second time until he had to flee from Jesus Christ. Very often, as believers, we want to fight the devil, and indeed we should, but we often make a critical mistake: we fight Satan at the same level at which he is tempting us. Those who are in the flesh cannot please God. If we try to fight Satan in the flesh, we will become victims of the devil.

The secret of true, successful, and strategic prayer against the lies in fighting at a higher spiritual level. Satan is our subject; therefore, he must be subjected by the authority of Christ to the level of a created creature; pitiful and wretched. Satan must look at you and see that you stand at a higher spiritual level. You are seated in the heavenly places together with Christ (Eph.2.6). He must see that you are above him and he cannot touch you.

You must become wiser and shrewder if you are going to defeat Satan when you enter into prayer. God has given me the ministry and gift of being an intercessor. I am not writing from mere sense knowledge; I am writing as an intercessor who spends countless hours praying. My life is a life of prayer. I am not telling you what I have simply heard; I am telling you what I know and live. It is what I know and what I do every day. I believe that as you open your heart while reading this book, the fire and burden of prayer will ignite within you.

Jeremiah had a passionate and extraordinary experience when he received a surge of God's fire. It is recorded in Jeremiah 20.9: "Then I said, 'I will not make mention of Him, Nor speak anymore in His name.' But His word was in my heart like a burning fire Shut up in my bones; I was weary of holding it back, And I could not." This is what has happened to me, literally. There are times when I feel tired and want to sleep, but the fire in my bones begins to burn, and I cannot sleep; I find myself praying. I cannot hold it back.

As you read this book, I want to promise you something by the power of the Holy Spirit: you are going to catch the fire of prayer. The fire of prayer will consume you. The fire will burn like acid in your heart, and your whole body will be aflame with spiritual fire. An impartation is taking place as you read this book, and your prayer life will never be the same again.

Remember, there are no riches greater than the riches of a complete and mature prayer life. I want to be rich in prayer, and I know I will be rich in everything. Prayer is an oasis; a well that never runs dry. Your life can never be dry if you keep it rooted in prayer.

However, it is not just prayer; it is not business as usual. Think again. Prayer requires preparation and planning. Do you plan before you pray? If you fail to plan, you are planning to fail. As Jeremiah 29.11 says, "For I know the thoughts that I think toward you, says the Lord, thoughts of peace and not of evil, to give you a future and a hope." Before God created humanity, He had a plan for what we would look like and the power we would possess.

In Genesis 1.26, we read, "Then God said, 'Let Us make man in Our image, according to Our likeness; let them have dominion over the fish of the sea, over the birds of the air, and over the cattle, over all the earth and over every creeping thing that creeps on the earth.'" God had a plan before He created humanity. He did not create us and then try to formulate a plan. Everything was meticulously thought out and put in order by God before it was done. Likewise, prayer requires careful planning if it is to be productive and effective.

In this book, I will show you how to plan your prayers so that God will answer them. Prayer is a battle. If you have not seen prayer this way, you need to change your perspective and understand prayer as a battle from today onward. Seeing prayer in this way will help you understand why you must carefully plan before you pray. Every time you engage in prayer, two armies are fighting: the army of God on the right and the army of Satan on the left. As an intercessor, you must see yourself as the general in God's army, directing the battle. You need to sit down and carefully plan how you will fight this battle. No army general would plunge into battle without a plan. No matter how skilled he is, if he neglects to plan, he sows the seeds of defeat. Think about this: prayer requires careful preparation and planning.

True and seasoned prayer warriors are like experienced army generals. They are unwilling to go to battle without adequate planning and preparation. They know battles are a matter of life and death. Meticulous and well-crafted planning is needed and must be made before entering into battle.

Have you taken the time to consider the direction of your prayers? "Ask, and it will be given to you; seek, and you will find; knock, and it will be opened to you. For everyone who asks receives, and he who seeks finds, and to him who knocks it will be opened" (Matt. 7.7-8).

These are the words of Jesus Himself. God desires to answer your prayers. He is waiting for you to bring your petitions before Him, and for the sake of His Son, Jesus Christ, He will answer your prayers. In John 14.13-14, Jesus said to His disciples, "And whatever you ask in My name, that I will do, that the Father may be glorified in the Son. If you ask anything in My name, I will do it."

But you might ask, "I have prayed for many years, Prophet Tom, but I have not received an answer. If God answers prayer, why has He not answered me?" I repeat this point because it is crucial. Repetition is not burdensome to me but serves as a safeguard for you. Many people think they are praying, but what they are actually doing is simply voicing their desperate needs. They are desperate, anxious, worried, or under pressure, and words spill out of their mouths in response to that pressure, which they then call prayer. But is this the real prayer God is expecting from you?

Many people call on God only when they are under pressure or in a crisis. They may cite David, who said, "In my distress I called upon the Lord, And cried out to my God; He heard my voice from His temple, And my cry came before Him, even to His ears" (Ps. 18.6). They conclude, "There is nothing wrong with calling on God in distress; He must answer my prayer." However, the same David also said, "Evening and morning and at noon I will pray, and cry aloud, And He shall hear my voice" (Ps. 55.17). David was a consistent prayer warrior. The book of Psalms is filled with prayers that David made and recorded before God.

Reflect on what I am saying to you. As you prepare to enter into prayer and fasting, consider the rules of engagement that you need to observe and follow.

Before you pray, it is crucial that you heed my words. These words speak to you in both Spirit and Life (John 6.63).

Therefore whoever hears these sayings of Mine, and does them, I will liken him to a wise man who built his house on the rock: and the rain descended, the floods came, and the winds blew and beat on that house; and it did not fall, for it was founded on the rock. 'But everyone who hears these sayings of Mine, and does not do them, will be like a foolish man who built his house on the sand: and the rain descended, the floods came, and the winds blew and beat on that house; and it fell. And great was its fall.' And so it was, when Jesus had ended these sayings, that the people were astonished at His teaching, for He taught them as one having authority, and not as the scribes." (Matt. 7.28-29)

Pay careful attention to this teaching; it will ultimately transform your prayer life and your entire life. Preparation and planning are essential components of effective fasting and prayer.

3

Where Do I Start

It is crucial to understand where to start when you embark on fasting and prayer. True prayer is prompted by the Holy Spirit; it must be ordered and directed by Him. Prayer should never be driven by your circumstances. What you are going through should not dictate the direction of your prayer. However, this is often the case. Pressure tends to prompt us to pray, often guiding the content of our prayers. For instance, if you are sick, you may find yourself praying for God to heal you. But what if this is not God's will?

The Apostle Paul provides an example of a prayer prompted by his own circumstances, recorded in 2 Corinthians 12.7-9: "And lest I should be exalted above measure by the abundance of the revelations, a thorn in the flesh was given to me, a messenger of Satan to buffet me, lest I be exalted above measure. Concerning this thing, I pleaded with the Lord three times that it might depart from me. And He said to me, 'My grace is sufficient for you, for My strength is made perfect in weakness.' Therefore most gladly I will rather boast in my infirmities, that the power of Christ may rest upon me."

Apostle Paul desperately wanted to be healed of his infirmity. His sickness was a significant challenge to both him and his ministry. Under pressure, he prayed, letting his needs guide his petition, but God did not grant his request. Through this, Paul learned that prayer must be prompted by the Holy Spirit. The Word of God confirms this: "The steps of a good man are ordered by the Lord, And He delights in his way" (Ps. 37.23).

Prayer prompted by our needs can be dangerous because it stems from the flesh. We cannot expect God to respond to the prompting of our flesh. God is Spirit, and those who worship Him must do so in spirit and in truth. Prayer, therefore, must be in the Spirit and grounded in the Word of God. As John 6.63 reminds us, "It is the Spirit who gives life; the flesh profits nothing."

Apostle Paul offers a compelling and instructive teaching on this matter in Romans 8.6-11: "For to be carnally minded is death, but to be spiritually minded is life and peace. Because the carnal mind is enmity against God; for it is not subject to the law of God, nor indeed can be. So then, those who are in the flesh cannot please God. But you are not in the flesh but in the Spirit, if indeed the Spirit of God dwells in you. Now if anyone does not have the Spirit of Christ, he is not His. And if Christ is in you, the body is dead because of sin, but the Spirit is life because of righteousness."

Before you enter into prayer, ensure you have taken sufficient time to meditate on the Word of God and prepare yourself spiritually. How do you do this? Find time to read the Word of God, slowly and reverentially. As you read, stop and ponder: Am I living according to what the Word of God says? Where am I falling short? How can I align myself with His Word? Confront your weaknesses head-on. Examine yourself to see whether you are still in the faith (2 Cor. 13.5).

Many believers are afraid to search themselves. It's easy to scrutinize others, but can you search yourself honestly and truthfully? King David was an extremely wise and godly man. His candidness and brokenness in the face of his human fragility were remarkable. He was a king with great power and authority, yet he understood that God is not concerned with your status. Whether you are a king or a slave, God expects you to walk with integrity. He expects you to search your inner self for any hidden faults or sins. David's sincerity in prayer is evident in Psalm 19.12: "Who can understand his errors? Cleanse me from secret faults." David knew how easy it is to see the sins of others, but it's another spiritual level when you can check yourself and say, "Lord, I am wrong here." When you reach that level, you are on your way to defeating the devil. The devil often hides in our pride and our unwillingness to search our hearts.

Get rid of sin

> Confess your trespasses to one another, and pray for one another, that you may be healed. The effective, fervent prayer of a righteous man avails much. Elijah was a man with a nature like ours, and he prayed earnestly that it would not rain; and it did not rain on the land for three years and six months. And he prayed again, and the heaven gave rain, and the earth produced its fruit. (Jas. 5.16-18)

Sin is the greatest hindrance to prayer. Sin obstructs prayer. Where there is sin, God will not intervene unless you are repenting. The prophet Isaiah provides deep insight into what sin does to prayer: "Behold, the Lord's hand is not shortened, that it cannot save; nor His ear heavy, that it cannot hear. But your iniquities have separated you from your God; and your sins have hidden His face from you, so that He will not hear" (Isa. 59.1-2). Sin damages our relationship with God and hinders our prayers. It is crucial, before we enter into prayer, to seek the face of God and check where we have grieved the Holy Spirit. Remember, the words I speak are both spirit and life.

Effective Prayer

Prayer is often taken for granted, yet it possesses immense power and possibilities. Prayer changes everything. It is communion with God, drawing us closer to Him. This is how powerful prayer is; it brings you into the presence of God. In this life and in the life to come, nothing can compare with the presence of God. This is what prayer does: it takes those who are far off from God and draws them near to Him. When you truly pray, it doesn't just bring you closer to God; it takes you right into His presence.

True prayer also recognizes the worthlessness of man and the worthiness of God. In true prayer, one casts away pride and clothes oneself in humility. When one's heart is burdened with pride, it is evident that one is talking to oneself, not to God. In Luke 18, we see two men praying. In verse 11, one man prays, saying, "God, I thank You that I am not like other men; extortioners, unjust, adulterers, or even as this tax collector. I fast twice a week; I give tithes of all that I possess." This man's prayer was full of his self-worth. Such a prayer cannot reach heaven.

In verse 13, we read: "And the tax collector, standing afar off, would not so much as raise his eyes to heaven, but beat his breast, saying, 'God, be merciful to me a sinner!'" Our Lord Jesus Christ examined the attitudes of the two men in their prayers and concluded, "I tell you, this man went down to his house justified rather than the other; for everyone who exalts himself will be humbled, and he who humbles himself will be exalted" (Luke 18.14).

I urge you, by the mercies of God, that in view of His grace, never neglect the discipline of prayer mixed with humility. Let your prayer rise up before the throne of God early in the morning. Psalms 5.3 says, "My voice You shall hear in the morning, O Lord; in the morning I will direct it to You, and I will look up." In Psalms 119.147, the psalmist declares, "I rise before the dawning of the morning, and cry for help; I hope in Your word."

Every genuine born-again Christian must practice waking up early in the morning to pray. Call upon God in the quietness and stillness of the morning, and you will hear wonderful things from the Lord. Give God your prime time, your undivided attention in the morning.

Remember, He is waiting for you every morning. He wants to hear your voice exalting His holy name. He is waiting to hear you magnify His name and praise Him for His goodness and mercy.

In Jeremiah 33.3, God says, "Call to Me, and I will answer you, and show you great and mighty things, which you do not know." In true prayer, one discovers their real value, their true worth. Prayer is a journey of discovery. By persistently praying, you will discover things you never knew about your life, your family, or your destiny.

Our prayer going forward should be a profound and transformative experience. Many people will discover the lost treasures in their lives; the unknown potential and opportunities Satan had hidden from their eyes by making them focus on negative things. You will uncover hidden revelations and secrets that will turn around your life, career, destiny, business, material life, and financial life for the glory of God.

As you engage in prayer, remember that faith energizes your prayer. Faith quickens your prayer. It's not just prayer; it is the prayer of faith that moves God. Faith moves God into action. If you want to see God in action in your life, release your faith. No matter how big the battle you are facing, faith provokes God. God is yearning to see a believer full of faith.

Of all the divine graces, the prayer of faith mixed with love possesses the power to withstand any pressure. This type of prayer can destroy any stronghold in your life and change any situation. The prayer of faith, when prompted by love, can open doors that seemed impossible to unlock; it can bring an end to the misery, disappointments, setbacks, and failures that have plagued many generations. Such a prayer will elicit an extraordinary response from God. It is also the kind of prayer that will help you maintain your integrity when faced with the pressure of sin and temptation. Therefore, do not neglect the prayer of faith mixed with love.

This kind of prayer, as I have mentioned before, carries immense power and possesses the ability to deeply impact and transform human life. Practice it, and you will walk in a victorious Christian life. Neglect it, and you will find yourself living an empty, frustrating, and disappointing existence; much like the unraveling portrayed in Chinua Achebe's *Things Fall Apart*.

4

The Burden that precedes true Prayer

We have often heard people say, "I have a burden for something." But what does this mean? How important is it to have a burden when one is praying? Can you pray effectively without a burden? In this chapter, we will explore these important questions that have puzzled and troubled humanity for many centuries.

The word "burden" in Greek is *baros*, meaning the weight of something, an onus, an encumbrance, or a load. The Greek word used for burden literally refers to the troubles of this life. The Bible describes the burden the prophet saw in Habakkuk 1.2-4. God has a burden to see humanity saved, which is why He sent His only begotten Son, Jesus Christ, to die on the cross. Through Jesus Christ, the burden of the yoke of sin might be broken so that believers might fulfil their purpose in life.

In Matthew 23.4-5, Jesus Christ warns the people against the scribes, Pharisees, and teachers of the law: "For they bind heavy burdens, hard to bear, and lay them on men's shoulders; but they themselves will not move them with one of their fingers. But all their works they do to be seen by men." Jesus Christ also says in Matthew 11.28-30, "Come to Me, all you who labour and are heavy laden, and I will give you rest. Take My yoke upon you and learn from Me, for I am gentle and lowly in heart, and you will find rest for your souls. For My yoke is easy and My burden is light."

When God gives us a burden for something, He does not intend to destroy us or take advantage of us. Rather, through the burden, God wants to prompt or enable us to act with deep conviction and urgency. This is when we cease to do things merely for the sake of doing them. The burden gives meaning and weight to what we are doing for the Lord. We become restless, pushed to act, and accomplish something for the Lord.

Moses felt the weight of the burden of the assignment God had given him. It was heavy on him. The assignment had great weight that came over his life. In Numbers 11.11, Moses said to the Lord, "Why have You afflicted Your servant? And why have I not found favour in Your sight, that You have laid the burden of all these people on me?" Moses felt the weight of the assignment, which was too difficult for a human being to carry. In Jeremiah 23.33 (ESV), it is written, "When one of this people, or a prophet or a priest asks you, 'What is the burden of the Lord?' you shall say to them, 'You are the burden, and I will cast you off, declares the Lord.'" As children of God, we can easily become a burden to the Lord when we do not mature, when we are murmuring and complaining, and when we are not being useful to the Lord. God is troubled by our lives.

In this book, however, we will focus on the burden that prompts one to act and to do something. Our world is writhing under the weight of burdens: homelessness, prostitution, the proliferation of wars and nuclear weapons that threaten to end human life as we know it. Poverty, disease, and drug problems spare no part of the world. We can talk about the globalization of human suffering and the growing threat to human dignity. The obscenity of the rich and corrupt stands in stark contrast to the suffering of the rest of the world. We have freedom fighters who are a threat to freedom itself. We have priests, prophets, and pastors who are purveyors of sin, and politicians who have corrupted the art of politics and governance. We too have governments without governance. These are the children of the 21st-century generation. Our conferences to bring peace often end in war. Our church sermons and fasting result in strife, quarreling, and striking each other with unclean fists.

I am given to meditation and critical thinking. My weakness is that I often think a lot about how we got here and how we can get out of here. This is the burden of the 21st century. But the burden God is giving us is another kind of burden. It is a burden that can move mankind to summon the courage to right past wrongs and extricate humanity from the clutches of the devil. How can we do this? What is the way? Which path should we take?

The psalmist says in Psalms 23, "The Lord is my shepherd; I shall not want. He makes me to lie down in green pastures; He leads me beside the still waters. He restores my soul; He leads me in the paths of righteousness for His name's sake." The Lord must lead us. But what is the Lord leading us to? God is giving us a burden that can prompt or move us to act.

This is what happened to Nehemiah when he inquired about the state of Jerusalem from Hanani and the other men who had come back from Jerusalem. What he heard gave him a burden:

And they said to me, "The survivors who are left from the captivity in the province are there in great distress and reproach. The wall of Jerusalem is also broken down, and its gates are burned with fire." So it was, when I heard these words, that I sat down and wept, and mourned for many days; I was fasting and praying before the God of heaven. And I said: "I pray, Lord God of heaven, O great and awesome God, You who keep Your covenant and mercy with those who love You and observe Your commandments, please let Your ear be attentive and Your eyes open, that You may hear the prayer of Your servant which I pray before You now, day and night, for the children of Israel Your servants, and confess the sins of the children of Israel which we have sinned against You. Both my father's house and I have sinned. We have acted very corruptly against You, and have not kept the commandments, the statutes, nor the ordinances which You commanded Your servant Moses" (Nehemiah 1.3-7).

Nehemiah's reaction to the news about Jerusalem reflects the deep burden he felt. He was profoundly moved. His immediate response was one of mourning, fasting, and praying as he sought God's guidance and mercy for the people of Israel. God gave him a burden to rebuild the walls of Jerusalem. As a result of this burden, he fasted and prayed. In Nehemiah 1:4, we read, "So it was, when I heard these words, that I sat down and wept, and mourned for many days; I was fasting and praying before the God of heaven."

This is the key point I want to emphasize: real, true, and effective prayer can only happen when you have received a burden. Your prayer ceases to be just a ritual; it becomes a powerful, compelling force driven by the Lord, urging you to both pray and act. "Faith without works is dead" (Jas. 2.26). Many of our prayers are merely ritualistic, self-serving, and lack a genuine burden. Sometimes, they are empty because there is nothing substantial behind them. Nehemiah wanted to remove the shame and disgrace from his people.

Have you ever found yourself struggling in prayer? Ask yourself this question: do you have a burden? You cannot pray effectively unless you have received a burden from the Lord. We often complain that our prayer meetings feel long because we do not have a burden. There is nothing propelling us to pray as intercessors. I have learned that the times I have prayed long, substantive prayers were when I had a burden. Now that I am more mature in the Lord and have developed a solid prayer ministry, I do not rush into prayer. Each morning, I first search for a burden. What do I want God to accomplish through my prayer? How important is that matter to me?

A burden is like gasoline to a car; it fuels a prayer that runs continuously. As Paul says, prayer without ceasing is based on a specific burden. The Lord must place a burden in your heart before He can move your heart to pray. Without a burden, it's common to see people on their phones, on Facebook, or WhatsApp during prayer meetings. They are often distracted because there is no burden. Pray that the Lord will give you a burden, and you will pray differently and effectively.

5

Impartation as a means to effective prayer

> Prayer is not an attempt to get what we want, but an endeavour to give God an opportunity to do what He wants through us. Prayer is not begging from God, but cooperating with Him. The thing to be sought is not how to get our way, but how to accept the will of God. The intent is not to change God's mind, but to change our attitudes. Prayer is really thinking in God's presence. As the level of our conscience is raised towards the level of God's thoughts, the happenings of life are seen in their truer perspective. Effective prayer involves a deep yearning to know God, an eagerness to trust God all the way, an ability to relinquish our hold, and a willingness to let go and let God. (McElroy 1961)

The temptation to view prayer like a fishing expedition is great and challenging in the 21st-century church. The true perspective of prayer is often lost, and consequently, the discipline of effective prayer has been thrown away in the maze of human desperation and depravity. We are drifting far from God, totally disconnected from His will and purpose for our lives. But prayer, when properly handled, is a lethal weapon in the mouths of believers to change the course of human history. Our generation, unlike others, stands at a crossroads;

we have lost the ancient path, the good way described in Jeremiah 6.16. James warns us that we do not receive answers to our prayers because we ask with wrong motives, so that we may spend what we receive on our pleasures (Jas 4.1-3).

Prayer is work; it's the work of aligning our lives with the will of the Lord. God is a God of order; there is no misalignment in Him. It is humanity, through sin and rebellion, that has distanced itself from God and needs to realign itself to become acceptable before Him. As the psalmist says, "Let the words of my mouth and the meditation of my heart be acceptable in Your sight, O Lord, my strength and my Redeemer" (Ps. 19.14). This realignment allows us to qualify to receive His good and precious promises for our lives. The goal of an intercessor must not only be to pray but to learn to pray effectively for the glory of God. God's glory must manifest itself through our prayer life.

In this chapter, I want to share what I have learned about the power of impartation in making prayer effective and life-changing. My understanding of impartation is deeply rooted in my experience, which has taught me that it is vital for jumpstarting a prayer life and developing it into one that is effectual and powerful. Experience, as they say, is the best teacher, and this has been true since time immemorial.

Paul, in the book of Romans, writes, "For I long to see you, that I may impart to you some spiritual gift, so that you may be established—that is, that I may be encouraged together with you by the mutual faith both of you and me" (Rom. 1.11-12). In the Old Testament, we are told of Moses in Numbers 11.24-25: "So Moses went out and told the people the words of the Lord, and he gathered seventy men of the elders of the people and placed them around the tabernacle. Then the Lord came down in the cloud, and spoke to him, and took of the Spirit that was upon him, and placed the same upon the seventy elders; and it happened, when the Spirit rested upon them, that they prophesied, although they never did so again."

God took some of the Spirit that had been given to Moses and placed it upon the seventy elders, so they would have the same spirit Moses had. Joshua, the son of Nun, received the spirit of wisdom because Moses had laid his hands on him, imparting that spirit to him. Impartation means the transfer of power, gift, anointing, or authority from one person to another. This is a mystery, a mastery of God's mysterious ways. Impartation is an act of faith and trust, happening in the realm of faith and trust. Many believers fail to receive from God because of doubt and unbelief. Our generation seems suffocated by the flesh, making it rare to find men and women of faith today.

It seems to me that men and women of faith have vanished from Christendom since the 18th and 19th centuries. Now, it appears that the Church of God is dominated by the flesh. Christians are no longer people of faith, but are instead driven by emotions rather than the Spirit of God. However, in the midst of this spiritual desert, I have opened my heart to the possibility of the power of God; that God is real, alive, and still at work. The Word of God declares that Jesus Christ, the Word made flesh who dwelt among us, is the same yesterday, today, and forever" (Heb. 13.8). The God who is revealed as alive and living in the Scriptures is indeed alive and living if you choose to believe in Him.

The incredible story of the father of a demon-possessed boy, who said, "Lord, I believe; help my unbelief!" (Mark 9.24), is still relevant today. Not long ago, we had just left the United Kingdom after being commanded by God to leave that country and set out for Canada. We obeyed, but found ourselves in Botswana on route to Canada. I had resolved not to beg for any offerings for my upkeep and that of my family. I needed time to start and establish a business. The business started well, but one month and two weeks after its inception in Gaborone, Botswana, the warehouse caught fire and destroyed everything. I did not have insurance, and that was the end of my story. In just one night, I became a poor man, and my life was thrown into a deep valley of confusion and desperation.

What compounded the situation was that my passport had expired. My wife and two children left for Canada, and I was stuck in Botswana. A month passed without any solution. During the second month, one day, I cried out to the Lord and prayed harder than I had ever prayed before. After my prayer, God spoke to me, saying, "Leave with your expired passport, and I will show you that I am the Lord." I thought I was losing my mind, but the voice repeated itself two or three times, and I instantly knew it was the voice of God.

When I called my wife to share this, she was shocked and thought I was losing my mind. I told her that I had heard from the Lord and needed to obey. Though it was a struggle, we eventually agreed that she would keep quiet and pray as I took this step of faith and trusted God. "For we walk by faith, not by sight" (2 Cor. 5.7) became not just a verse but a real command of the Lord, a word for the present moment, a "now" word for me.

On the day I left Botswana, a group of 20 church members came to see me off. None of them knew I had a problem with my passport. Faith is a personal conviction and trust; it resides within you and in your heart. Sometimes, people make the mistake of sharing their dreams with unbelievers; those who do not believe that God still performs miracles today.

What happened at Sir Seretse Khama International Airport was unbelievable; an act of faith. I boarded the plane with an expired passport. I landed at Oliver Tambo International Airport and passed through six checkpoints, yet no one noticed that my passport was expired. What blew my mind was that my flight was going via JFK International Airport in New York, one of the most secure airports in the world, yet no one detected that my passport had expired. That is how I came to Canada.

I am not sure if such faith still exists in our generation, but whether people believe it or not, God is real and performs wonders. This truth has guided my walk of faith in God. I have refused to limit God by my personal fears and doubts. Faith is rational only to a believing heart. It is out of a man's heart, not of a man's mind. For faith to be understood, your heart must speak to your mind. Many believers make the mistake of wanting their minds to speak to their hearts. No, the heart is greater than the mind. Your heart must be in the right place for it to command your mind to believe the Word of God.

I now return to the essence of this chapter: the discovery of how spiritual impartation takes place. We have examined several scriptures demonstrating that spiritual impartation is biblical and well-supported by evidence in the Word. The Bible clearly teaches that "iron sharpens iron" (Prov. 27.17). In other words, one believer can strengthen another in their spiritual giftings. It takes a humble servant of God to recognize the gifts in another and to desire that God would work through that stronger believer, who is stronger in a particular are or gifting, to impact the life of a believer who may not have, or is weaker in that area or gifting.

In our spiritual walk, the spirit of pride and self-righteousness is a significant hindrance to impartation. Many people say, "I only need God; I do not need another person to lay hands on me. God will do it Himself." Unfortunately, many Christians have suffered spiritual shipwreck due to such pride. Today, in the body of Christ, we often fail to value one another as members of the same body; Christ. The Word of God commands us to submit to one another out of reverence for Christ (Eph. 5.21). Impartation allows us to empower and encourage one another as the body of Christ, working together for the glory of God.

I am grateful that I have not only read about impartation in the Bible but have personally experienced its power. Around June 2003, I attended a prayer meeting led by an Apostle in Forward in Faith International (ZAOGA). I was hungry for the gift of prayer, having just discovered its power and having read many books on prayer by E.M. Bounds. I wanted to learn how to pray effectively.

In that meeting, which took place in Birmingham, I met an Apostle of prayer. I listened intently to every teaching and imitated the man of God, making sure he saw how hungry and desperate I was for a touch from God. I wanted to pray differently. At the end of the prayer meeting, he singled me out, laid his hands on me, and immediately the fire of prayer fell upon me. A surge of power and a mighty burden for prayer overwhelmed me. I returned home to Coventry, excited and happy, praying that night like never before.

The next morning, we headed back to Birmingham for a provincial Sunday service, where about 1,000 people had gathered. The overseer tried to lead the prayer, but it was dry and difficult; no one seemed interested in praying. As an elder in the church, I was called upon by the overseer to take over. When I took the microphone, the anointing of God came upon me mightily, and I began to lead the prayer. Suddenly, a tsunami of God's power fell upon the auditorium, and the Holy Spirit moved among the people. The fire of prayer ignited the entire congregation. We pressed on in prayer, and I only realized afterward that we had prayed for an hour and a half. Everyone was shocked, yet so excited. From that day on, my prayer life and my influence on prayer have been remarkable. This transformation only happened through impartation.

6

The Evidence of the power of prayer

In our generation, people talk about God but do they really know God? In Jeremiah 33.3, God says, "'Call to Me, and I will answer you, and show you great and mighty things, which you do not know.'" What things can we say came from God? In this book, The Man and His God, Prophet Tom Tirivangani shows us that God is real. He is not an abstract God, but a living and life-changing God.

In this book we are introduced to God who is alive and living. These are stories of real people who have encountered God through the ministry of Prophet Tom Tirivangani. I am constantly challenged when I read the bible, Moses parted the red sea with a stick, Joshua made the sun stand still, Gideon made the sun go backwards 10 times, and Peter's shadow healed the sick. My question is, where is the God of the bible? Where has He gone? Where is He hiding? Sure, enough God has shown me that he is the same yesterday, today and forever.

Let me narrate what happened to me in 2007. My passport expired while I was in Botswana, my wife and children left for Canada and I was left; stuck in Gaborone Botswana. I tried to renew my passport but there was no joy and no result. I fasted and prayed, one day I prayed and groaned for hours looking for an answer from God. I got tired and fell asleep in the secret place I was praying. God gave me a revelation in a dream. He took me to the passport office and showed me all that the enemy was doing to block my passport from being released. God said to me in the dream, "If you trust me take your passport and go to Canada and I will show you that I am God". I thought I was getting crazy but this was the word of God. I called my wife Colline and explained to her what God had told me. She disagreed and said I was acting irrationally and that I would get into trouble by travelling on an expired passport, but I was not willing to disobey God. I knew in my inner heart that I had heard the voice of God clearly.

I went to the travel agent and rebooked my ticket. On the day of my flight, I went to Sir Seretse Khama International Airport and checked in without anyone noticing my passport had expired. I flew to Johannesburg in South Africa. At Olive Tambo International Airport, I had six checkpoints but no one noticed that my passport had expired. As if God wanted me to know that He was real, I went through JFK International Airport in New York in the United States. There airport officials and immigration could not see that my passport had expired.

This is the God who brought me to Canada. When I finally settled in Hamilton, I became troubled and disillusioned. I said, "God why did you bring me here to Canada where everyone seems to know you?" God answered me and said, "Wait I will show you what you have never seen."

One day God woke me up from 301-15 Albright Road and said, "Come now let me show you why I brought you here". God has a way he deals with me. I have a close and intimate relationship with Him. I have the greatest privilege of hearing His voice. I got into my car He directed me until I came to the corner of Gage Avenue and King Street in Hamilton. There was a Tim Hortons coffee shop there. I saw a young lady about 24 or 25 years old who had a baby in a stroller. I approached her and tried to witness to her but she angrily told me that she was a witch and was not interested in Christianity.

In these stories, I present to you the wonder-working God whom I serve. Enjoy reading the stories of God's miraculous power and be inspired to believe God for more.

Supernatural encounters

Evangelist Farai Gwata

Sometime in 2016, Prophet Tom, a member of the Media team, and I went to an electronics store to purchase cameras for the Media team. There was nothing outwardly distinctive about Prophet Tom. We were all dressed modestly in jeans and T-shirts, with unkempt hair. At the time, many of us close to the Prophet tended to imitate his appearance, as he felt led to grow his hair and not comb it often, so we followed suit.

When we entered the store, we were attended to by a gentleman who was a Sikh. He was dressed in his turban and other religious regalia. As he began assisting us, we let him know we were looking for a camera for the church. The Media team member and I were the most vocal, appearing to know exactly what we wanted.

In all physical appearances, Prophet Tom seemed distant, uninterested, and perhaps even unknowledgeable about the purpose of our visit. He wandered around the store, quietly looking at various pieces of equipment. To any observer, it would have seemed that Prophet

Tom had merely accompanied two individuals who knew what they were doing.

This is why we were astonished when the Sikh attendant walked right past the two of us and went directly to Prophet Tom. Looking at him intently, the man said, "Man of God, please tell me more about your church so I can help you get the right equipment."

I was stunned. Addressing the store attendant, I asked how, out of the three of us, he had recognized that Prophet Tom was the man of God. Our Sikh friend replied, "I am a spiritual man, and I can identify another spiritual man. It doesn't take a genius to perceive that he," nodding toward Prophet Tom; "is a spiritual being."

Despite all physical appearances, this attendant accurately discerned that Prophet Tom was the man of God, even though he seemed the most detached among us.

Pastor Sarah Craig

A Journey to the Secret Place

My name is Sarah Greig, and I was introduced to CVR by my daughter, Tino Kasi, in 2022.

I initially sought a stamp of approval from the Man of God (MOG) for a relationship I was uncomfortable with. When I didn't receive the approval, I decided to attend a service. One service turned into many. I thought I already knew about the MOG from Forward in Faith many years ago, but the more I listened to his preaching, the more I became aware that his teachings represented an entirely different doctrine.

Before CVR, I had been attending a Pentecostal church in London, but my few services at CVR challenged my beliefs and approach to worship. I realized that Prophet Tom took his interactions with God seriously, whereas I did not. I spoke in tongues on Sundays but lived the life of an unbeliever throughout the week. The truth is, I didn't even know what the life of a believer looked like. I had created my own way of living; a way that was not aligned with God's Word. Prophet Tom's life reflected something entirely different.

This led me to reflect on the Scripture: "There is a way that seems right to a man, but its end is the way of death" (Prov. 14.12). I became curious about what Prophet Tom had discovered concerning life. To this day, I remain curious, and I find myself wanting more of what he has experienced. One thing I know for sure is that I must be willing to exchange my life for that of Jesus Christ so that I may live His life.

This exchange, however, requires a great deal of chiselling; much like bricks are chiselled to be fit for building a house. The process is not comfortable, but the more I experience Jesus, the more I love pleasing Him, and the less I want to grieve Him. I am now on a journey where my greatest wish is "to dwell in the secret place of the Most High" (Ps. 91.1). At that place lies everything I have ever sought in life: healing, joy, and peace.

Prophet Tom appears to have discovered how to access that place; through prayer, prayer, prayer, and prayer: the four cornerstones of this ministry. Prophet Tom cannot take you there; it is up to you to make the decision to follow the direction given by the Man of God. You must choose to *"abide in the secret place of the Most High"* and then avail yourself to Him. Only then can you experience the real life in Jesus Christ, rather than merely talking about Him.

A Divine Intervention in the Parking Lot

Back in 2015, CVR Ministries owned and operated a thrift store. One day, as we were leaving for the day, we noticed a woman standing next to her vehicle, which was parked with its hood open in the parking lot opposite the thrift store. Prophet Tom approached her and asked if everything was all right.

The woman responded that all was not well; she had been stuck there all afternoon, unable to start her car. She explained how several people, including mechanics, had stopped to help but eventually left humiliated, advising her to call a tow truck and have her car inspected by professional technicians.

The man of God then said, "Oh, okay, go ahead and close the hood." Not knowing what the Prophet had in mind, I closed the hood. He then said, "Now, let's push the car out of the parking lot and into the street."

Brother Thabo and I, both engineering students at the time, exchanged looks. Without saying a word, we communicated the same thought: Did we just hear that? Push an automatic car into the street? Mechanics had already come and left embarrassed, the car is safe in the parking lot, and now the man of God wants to complicate matters further by pushing it into the street!

We both froze, unsure of what to do. Finally, we observed the Prophet himself getting ready to push the car. I reasoned in my heart, No matter how crazy this seems, I can't let him push the car by himself. So, I reluctantly joined him but decided not to use all my strength;

I wanted to save some energy for pushing the car back into the parking lot.

When the car was finally in the street, the man of God turned to me and instructed, "Start the car."

Again, I froze. A million thoughts raced through my mind. I didn't want to embarrass the Prophet, but I was also convinced this would not work. Sensing my hesitation, the man of God gently stepped forward and said, "Okay, let me start the car myself."

At that moment, I felt a sickening sensation in my stomach. There we were, in the middle of the street, with a crowd beginning to gather to watch the scene unfold. I thought for sure that the Prophet was about to make fools out of all of us. In my internal turmoil, the sounds of street chatter and passing cars suddenly faded into silence.

I was jolted back to reality by the loud roaring of an engine. I looked up to see the Prophet standing next to the car, signalling to the woman to get in and drive home safely. He calmly assured her that she didn't need to worry about taking the car to a mechanic; it was now permanently fixed.

Even five years later, I can vividly recall the young woman's reaction. She stood there, trembling like a reed, hesitant to step inside her car. Finally, she managed to muster enough strength to utter three words as she stared at the Prophet and the idling car: "Who are you?"

Shamese Fletcher

Speaking with Angels

It was during the *15 Days of Prayer & Fasting 2020*, and I had retired to the assigned rooms with the other mothers and young babies after the morning prayer session. The evening session was scheduled to start around 6:00 or 6:30 p.m. As I rested, drifting into light sleep, one of my sisters, a fellow mother, appeared at the door.

I distinctly remember that she was dressed in the same clothes she had been wearing in the morning, with one difference: she now wore a headscarf. She addressed me in a serious and concerned tone, saying, "What are you doing? What are you doing?"

At first, I thought she was reprimanding me for sleeping before the evening prayer session, perhaps suggesting I should have been praying without ceasing. I glanced at my phone to check the time, which showed 5:30 p.m., and replied, "We still have a little time."

She looked at me with serious, reddish eyes before leaving. Despite her intense expression, I brushed it off and went back to sleep.

When it was time for the evening prayer, I joined the session. During the prayer, an elder approached me and asked if I knew where the same sister was. Confidently, I replied that she was around, as I had just spoken to her.

A few hours later, I saw her entering the prayer meeting, coming from outside. Surprised, I asked her why she had woken me up earlier. To my astonishment, she responded, "I went home after the afternoon prayer and just arrived now for the evening session."

I was shocked and began to doubt my own reality. Could I have imagined it? Even if it were a dream, it felt far too vivid and detailed to dismiss. The experience left me uneasy. Seeking clarity, I decided to approach my Spiritual Father, Prophet Tom and relayed to him what had happened.

He listened attentively and said, "I will explain after the prayer." When the prayer concluded, he told me, "It was an angel who appeared to you, but it came in a friendly form so you wouldn't be afraid."

Reflecting on this experience, I am overwhelmed by the love of the God of Prophet Tom. He is so caring, and I feel honoured and important to Him.

Evangelist Keena Gwata

Angelic Reception

One day around 5 a.m., I heard a voice instructing me to go to the servant of God's home. His home wasn't far from ours, so I immediately woke up Brother Marius. We packed our bags and walked to Prophet Tom's house.

When we arrived, we were shocked to find Prophet Tom already outside, as though he had been expecting us. He greeted us with, "Good morning. The Lord told me He was sending two angels." He then asked us to come along with him.

The Prophet handed us a broom and a rake and led us to an elderly man's house. The house was quite large, but the lawn was overgrown, with dead leaves and weeds scattered everywhere. The elderly man was outside, struggling to clean up.

Prophet Tom approached him, and we followed the Prophet's instructions as he directed us to help with the cleanup. For the next three hours, we worked alongside the elderly man, clearing the lawn and restoring its appearance.

After we finished, the elderly man expressed his heartfelt gratitude to Prophet Tom, saying he had been struggling for a long time with no one to help him.

Even now, I often wonder: How did Prophet Tom know we were coming? Why were we chosen to witness this? And how was Prophet Tom so active and intentional in his actions?

Despite my questions, I give all praise to God.

Pastor Errol Goodwin

Hem of Prophet's Garment

In the month of January 2021, we were having a 15-days of prayer and fasting.

During this time, we had 3 prayer sessions daily; 4 am, 11 am, and 6 pm. On this particular day, I woke up at 3:30 am which was earlier than usual, and I went to pray in the gym.

As I was lying down praying, the Man of God Prophet Tom entered the room and I could see one of his pants legs was tucked in his sock. I approached him and bent down to fix it. As soon as I touched his pants, I felt a power leave the Prophet's body and it shocked my whole body.

He has touched me many times before whether praying for me or shaking my hand, but this time was different, the anointing was super amazing, & and now I truly understand the story of the woman with the issue of blood. When she touched the hem of Jesus garment her life was impacted and changed for the glory of God.

Angels in the Service

Prophet Tom Tirivangani

In August 2020, during a Sunday live service, the Man of God, Prophet Tom, opened the service with prayer and declared, "Today, the Lord promised me that He would send angels to the service."

The Prophet of God then delivered the sermon with great power and conviction. During the time of prayer, the Prophet assured the congregation that the angels had arrived. The presence of God was thick and tangible throughout the service, filling the atmosphere with His glory.

Later, many members of the congregation came forward to testify that they had seen the angels during the service, affirming the Prophet's words and the divine encounter.

I was serving in the house of the Lord on August 30, 2020. I saw the prophet of God alone praying at the altar, when I looked I saw a large being with wings, flapping his wings on the altar where the Prophet was praying"

Brother Marek

I was in the church on August 30, 2020, and the prophet was praying, calling for the angels. I saw the sanctuary full of angels.

On August 30, 2020, I was attending church and I saw many angels surrounding the man of God, then they went from the Altar to the people.

Prophet Clearing the way!

The family that I was staying with invited me to their church and as a guest in someone's house I had no choice but to attend. After meeting with the man of God several times and having him pray for me and observing everything he did, I was in deep contemplation. Being a Christian and having my own church back home, I really wanted to know from God if Prophet Tom was for real. That is when I had the dream.

"I dreamt I was back at home, and the man of God Prophet Tom was with me. We were walking together in our path, and there appeared to be many obstacles, but in his right hand Prophet Tom was holding something that he was using to demolish everything in our way...so as we walked Prophet Tom would swing his hand in front of us, and clear the way so we could keep on moving"

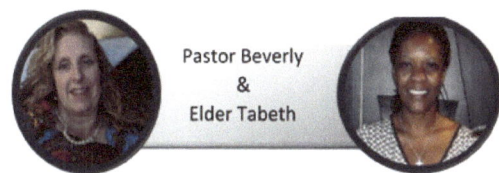

Smoke of Divine Presence

As we were preparing the house for the man of God where he would be staying when he arrived in Namibia or the Taste of Heaven Crusade, we had a powerful encounter.

I was in a room hanging curtains, when I looked across the hall to where Elder Tabeth was preparing the bedroom, I saw smoke rising upward from the floor. It looked as if my eyes were playing tricks on me. The smoke was still there, but I didn't smell any smoke, I just saw it.

I ran to the bedroom where the smoke was coming from and the room was filled with smoke. The moment I entered the room, I collapsed, fell to my knees, and started worshipping the God of Prophet Tom.

I looked over to my right and Elder Tabeth was on the floor and she started praying loudly, we were both soaked in God's thick presence and anointing and could not physically get up. I have never experienced that kind of anointing and presence in my life before.

Testimonies

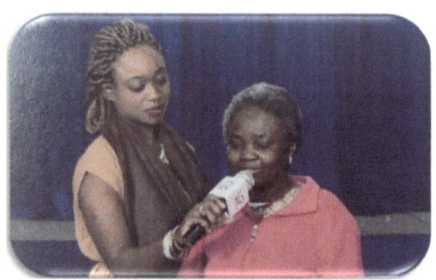

Healed of Cancer

Mama Ruth Stephens, after being diagnosed with cancer and undergoing a challenging battle with the illness, experienced a remarkable turn of events. During her hospital stay, she received a prophetic word from Prophet Tom, who prayed for her and declared that she was cancer-free. Miraculously, just three days later, multiple medical tests confirmed the Prophet's declaration, showing no trace of cancer cells in her body. Glory be to God for this incredible healing!

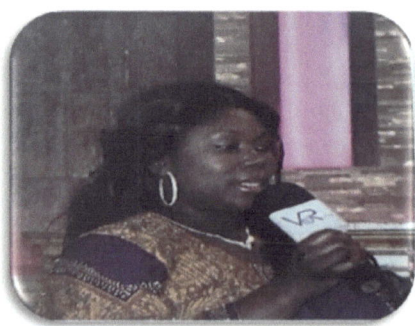

Another Cancerous Tumor Disappears

Mrs. Jarso Nzau gives glory to God for the miraculous removal of a brain tumour from her unborn child. Upon receiving the devastating news from their doctor that an ultrasound showed a brain tumour in the child she was carrying, the Nzau family sought serious prayer with the Man of God, Prophet Tom in combination with the anointing water "New Season". Through their faith and fervent prayers, a second ultrasound later confounded the doctors, revealing that the tumor had completely disappeared. Praise be to God for this wondrous healing! To God be the glory!

Never a sickness Jesus Cannot Heal: Infant with holes in the heart receives Healing

The baby was born with four holes in her heart. Following this diagnosis, the Man of God instructed the evangelists to go to the hospital, spray the anointing water on the child, and offer prayer. After following the Man of God's instructions, a miraculous healing occurred. The very next day, the baby was released from the hospital with three of the holes miraculously closed, and she was breathing on her own. To the glory of God, this remarkable event is a testament to the power of faith and prayer.

Woman Destined for Surgery Healed

After all medical procedures indicated that Ms. Joyce Belmont needed surgery, she attended the prayer line and received prayer from the servant of God, Prophet Tom, who assured her that she was healed. On the scheduled day of surgery, while she lay on the operating table, she experienced a miraculous moment. The surgeons surrounding her were unable to find any problem that required surgery. Imagine her joy and awe as she got off the surgeon's table, knowing that God had healed her. Glory be to God!

Dead Man Lives

Sis Sharon gives this amazing testimony! The doctor pronounced her fiancé dead, and they were prepared to pull the plug and switch off the life support machine. In desperation, she called the Man of God, Prophet Tom, who emphatically instructed that the life support machine must not be switched off until he said so. This caused much pandemonium at the hospital as the doctors went into consultation. Mean-

while, Prophet Tom went into his prayer chamber. Miraculously, the situation changed as all the machines suddenly started to read a heartbeat from the previously dead man. A few weeks later, Sharon and her fiancé walked out of the hospital together. Glory be to God for this incredible miracle!

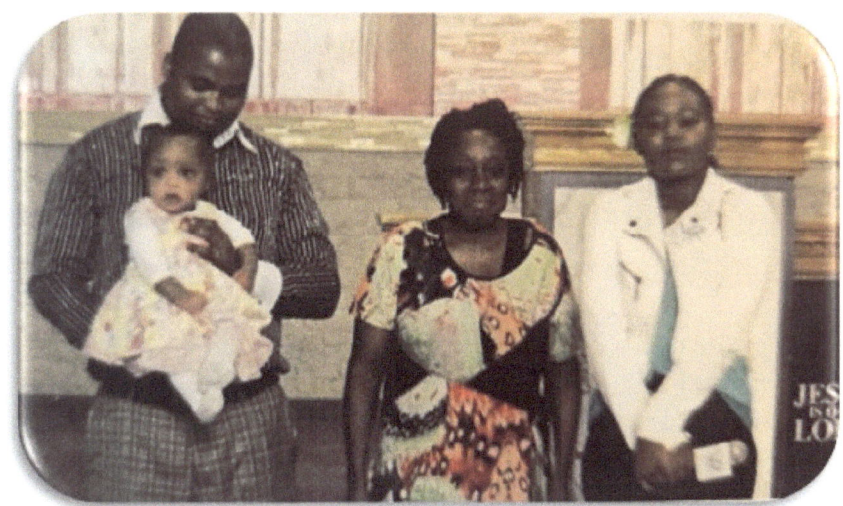

Woman with Fibroids Conceives

Mrs. Felicia Katso was told by doctors that she was unable to conceive or carry a pregnancy to term due to a severe fibroid condition. Desperately wanting children with her husband of five years, she sought help from the Man of God, Prophet Tom. He assured her, "It is well, God is faithful," and prophetically declared that she would give birth to a baby girl. Several months later, during a service, Prophet Tom called Mrs. Katso out and said, "When you come back from your trip there will be a big surprise for your husband." True to the Prophet's word, upon returning from her trip, she found out she was expecting. Today, Mr. and Mrs. Katso are the proud parents of a beautiful baby girl named Victoria. Glory be to God!

Immigration

Mrs. Marjorie Makwanzine shares her incredible testimony:

"I arrived in Canada in May 2015 as an asylum seeker. Six months later, I faced my immigration hearing; a moment that would determine my future. I had asked the Man of God, Prophet Tom, to be my witness. However, when the hearing began, he was nowhere to be seen.

As I stood before the court, things quickly took a turn for the worse. I was losing track of dates, stumbling over events, and struggling to make sense. My attorney, seeing how badly things were going, requested a recess.

Glory be to God! During that recess, Prophet Tom arrived. Despite being more than two hours late, the judge made an unprecedented decision—he allowed the Man of God to speak.

After Prophet Tom's testimony, the judge declared, 'Because of this man's testimony, I will grant you stay. I believe everything he has said. Your own story, on the other hand, made no sense at all.'

I will forever be grateful to God for using Prophet Tom, a man of prayer, to change my destiny that day. To God be the glory!"

20-Year Ear Infection Healed

Mr. Michael Chachana gives glory to God for his miraculous healing.

He testifies that he was given anointed water that had been prayed for by the Man of God, Prophet Tom. That very night, after administering the anointed water to his ear, he had a vision in his sleep. In the vision, he saw his ear being operated on before his very own eyes.

When he woke up the next morning, the ear infection and ailment he had suffered from since 1996 were completely gone!

Truly, the power of prayer is remarkable!

Delivered by Faith: A Sleepless Man's Miracle

Evangelist Vivian Akoi Swen shared a powerful testimony about a patient at her workplace who had been unable to sleep for two years, despite trying various sleep medications. While attending to this patient, he read the

"Faith Works with an Open Heart" booklet, written by the man of God, Prophet Tom. After reading the booklet and repeatedly stating, "There is something different about this man," while looking at

Prophet Tom's picture on the cover, the patient began to sleep soundly. The entire workplace is in awe of this miraculous transformation, praising God for using the booklet as a medium to deliver the man and restore his ability to sleep. Glory be to God!

From Epileptic to Healed, From Broken to Blessed: A Journey of Faith and Prayer

Testimonies remind us of God's boundless power to transform lives. This uplifting story follows a young woman who faced tremendous challenges but emerged victorious through faith and prayer. For years, she battled epilepsy, enduring frequent seizures that caused her to fall and lose control, even peeing on herself. The spirit of death loomed over her, and she relied on 104 tablets daily to manage her condition. Alongside her health struggles, she faced heartbreak when the enemy attacked and shattered her marriage.

Despite these overwhelming trials, she clung to her faith and continued to seek God's intervention. Her perseverance paid off in miraculous ways. Not only did she receive complete healing from epilepsy; no longer needing any medication; but God also blessed her with a new, loving marriage as she continued to focus on God, after the enemy had tried to destroy her joy.

Her story is a powerful testament to the incredible power of faith, prayer, and God's unwavering love. It shows that even in the darkest moments, God is able to restore, heal, and bless abundantly. Be encouraged and uplifted by her journey, which serves as a beacon of hope for anyone facing their own trials. With faith and perseverance, no obstacle is too great, and God's plans are always for our ultimate good.

Double Double Blessings

Sister Anita's journey is a powerful testimony of faith and obedience. Despite facing significant challenges, she remained steadfast in her commitment to tithing, fully understanding it as a key to breaking the curse of poverty.

Her faithfulness was rewarded in extraordinary ways: she received multiple promotions, her salary doubled within a year, and she was promoted to a higher position even before starting her new job.

Through her story, Sister Anita encourages others to trust in God's principles, emphasizing that while tithing may be difficult, it is a profound tool for breaking financial curses and unlocking doors to abundant blessings.

All glory to God for her double portion blessing!

From Days to Years: A Miraculous Healing

During the COVID-19 pandemic, Elder Pat, a nurse by profession, faced a life-altering diagnosis of stage 4 cancer. Her doctor delivered the devastating news: she had only three months to live. Although she had maintained a healthy lifestyle, the diagnosis shattered her world.

In her despair, Elder Pat bought a notebook from a dollar store to count down the days she believed remained—2 months and 16 days. Each day of intense pain reinforced her belief, *This is the pain that will take my life.*

But God had other plans. Elder Pat was referred to Christ Voice of Restoration Ministries. At the church, Prophet Tom spoke a prophetic word over her life, declaring that she would live and not die. Elder Pat clung to this declaration of faith and began attending the international prayer line at 4 am, 11 am, and 6 pm, even logging in during her chemotherapy sessions.

Through consistent prayer, personal intercession from Prophet Tom, and unshakable faith in the Word of God, a miracle unfolded. What was supposed to be three months has now turned into three years and counting.

All glory to God for this extraordinary testimony of healing, grace, and restoration!

7

Prayer: The Discipline That Transforms

"Discipline is the heart of progress" Prof. Tom Tirivangani

As I conclude this very important book on prayer, I cannot finish it without dealing with the subject of prayer and discipline. What role does discipline play in the call to effective prayer? I see it this way: the human heart is the seat of life, both physically and spiritually. Without the heart, the body has no life; it is merely an empty vessel. Now, consider this analogy: discipline is to prayer what the heart is to the body. Just as the body cannot function without the heart, a prayer life cannot exist without discipline. Where there is no discipline, prayer is dead. Without discipline, we cannot speak of an effective prayer life.

Moses spent forty days and forty nights on the mountain, waiting on God and speaking with Him (Exod. 34.28). It was discipline that kept him in prayer on the mountain for those forty days. Similarly, Jesus fasted for forty days and forty nights in the wilderness (Matt. 4.2). Such a feat in prayer required immense discipline. It was discipline that enabled Jesus Christ to overcome the devil's temptations at a time when His body was weak and vulnerable. Despite His exhaustion and hunger, He remained focused on His divine mission, refusing to let the devil distract Him with immediate personal needs.

Throughout His ministry, Jesus faced rejection and persecution from the Jewish Sanhedrin, yet He never allowed their attacks to distract him from the goal of delivering humanity from the bondage of Satan. From the betrayal by Judas Iscariot to the agony of the crucifixion at Golgotha, He maintained a level of discipline in prayer that is unparalleled in history. It is astonishing to consider that, even in His darkest hour, Jesus prayed for His enemies, demonstrating extraordinary dedication to the will of God (Luke 23.34).

Jesus began His ministry in prayer and sustained it through deep prayer. His devotion to prayer exemplifies the highest level of discipline and commitment to the Kingdom of God. In the hour of His greatest trial, He sought God in the Garden of Gethsemane (Matt. 26.36–39) and concluded His journey with a prayer on the cross at Calvary (Luke 23.46). What amazes and confounds me most is that, even in the midst of excruciating pain and humiliation, Jesus' discipline in prayer remained unbroken.

His ministry of prayer passed the test of discipline in two key ways: first, as self-control, and second, as focus, persistence, and the drive to achieve a fixed, divine goal. One might have expected the Son of Man to buckle under the weight of His suffering. Yet, He displayed a level of composure, courage, and magnanimity beyond human comprehension. When insulted and intimidated, the temptation to respond in strength was great; if He had been an ordinary man. They taunted Him; mortality mocked immortality, the creature insulted the Creator, weakness challenged strength, and lies provoked the Truth. Yet, our Lord and Saviour remained silent and serene, never panicking despite the atmosphere being charged with provocation.

It may help you, as the reader, to reflect on the events at the cross as recorded in the synoptic Gospels. I will focus on the account given by Luke, the physician. In Luke 23, many profound truths and revelations unfold before us. In the midst of suffering, Jesus demonstrated an unparalleled level of discipline, courage, and purity. Let us examine a couple of key moments that highlight His level of discipline and focus.

Luke records: "Then Herod, with his men of war, treated Him with contempt and mocked Him, arrayed Him in a gorgeous robe, and sent Him back to Pilate" (Luke 23.11). Almighty Jesus had the power to answer Herod and his soldiers, yet He remained silent. The depth of His quietness and serenity in the face of such mockery was shocking. This is what discipline can achieve when one knows who they are and what assignment God has given them.

Have you ever been tempted to change your prayers in the midst of persecution, feeling the urge to prove your power, anointing, and authority? Not so with Christ. Instead, He remained focused on His mission. In Luke 23.26–31, we read:

> Now as they led Him away, they laid hold of a certain man, Simon a Cyrenian, who was coming from the country, and on him they laid the cross that he might bear it after Jesus. And a great multitude of the people followed Him, and women who also mourned and lamented Him. But Jesus, turning to them, said, 'Daughters of Jerusalem, do not weep for Me, but weep for yourselves and for your children. For indeed the days are coming in which they will say, "Blessed are the barren, wombs that never bore, and breasts which never nursed!" Then they will begin to say to the mountains, "Fall on us!" and to the hills, "Cover us!"' (Luke 23.26–31).

For if they do these things in the green wood, what will be done in the dry? (Luke 23.31). I am greatly amazed at the response of our Lord Jesus Christ. Who would not want others to feel sorry for them when going through a dark moment? Yet Jesus said, "Weep not for Me, but for yourselves" (Luke 23.28). His mission and assignment were never altered.

Do the focus and intensity of your prayer change due to a lack of discipline and your immediate needs Do you compromise in prayer because the enemy has put you under pressure? Yet we see in Jesus an attitude of discipline, unbroken, unyielding, wholly determined, and resolute. If you mastered the act of discipline like Christ did, your prayer life will achieve milestones both for you and for humanity.

Yet our prayer sometimes grasps for breath and strength because we lack discipline in the final moments before his passing, Jesus demonstrated two remarkable acts, displays of rare discipline and love. He prayed, "Father, forgive them, for they do not know what they do" (Luke 23.34). Instead of seeking sympathy for himself, Jesus saw the wretchedness of humanity, its misguided zeal, and its utter ignorance. In humanity's weakest yet most arrogant moment, mankind claimed strength. Jesus could have crushed humanity once and for all. Instead, in the magnitude of his character, he extended forgiveness through prayer.

The last thing he did, as recorded in Scripture, is found in Luke 23.46–49:

> And when Jesus had cried out with a loud voice, He said, 'Father, into Your hands I commit My spirit.' Having said this, He breathed His last. So when the centurion saw what had happened, he glorified God, saying, 'Certainly this was a righteous Man!' And the whole crowd who came together to that sight, seeing what had been done, beat their breasts and returned. But all His acquaintances, and the women who followed Him from Galilee, stood at a distance, watching these things (Luke 23.46–49).

What a response. Even in his hour of trial, Jesus did not take matters into his own hands. How often, as human beings, do we feel compelled to take control, casting aside divine covering and abandoning our mission? From the time Jesus was questioned by his mother, Mary, about why he had stayed behind in the temple, his response remained consistent: "Did you not know that I must be about My Father's business?" (Luke 2.49). Later, he would affirm, "I do nothing of Myself" (John 8.28).

"What I see the Father do, so I do also" (John 5.19). At the end of his life, Jesus committed his spirit into the hands of his Father. We should learn valuable lessons from this in our prayer life. For prayer to be effective, it requires discipline to maintain focus and passion. If prayer is not to be altered by the pressures we face daily, it must be rooted in discipline. To keep prayer moving in one direction, it is important that discipline becomes part of the rubric of that prayer.

Jesus said in Luke 18.1, "Men always ought to pray and not lose heart." But how can one persevere in prayer when there is no immediate answer? How can one remain steadfast when the storms of life are overwhelming? It is only through mastering the art of discipline. Many of our prayers lack effectiveness, often becoming ritualistic and contaminated by personal needs, simply because we lack discipline.

Jesus said in Matthew 26.40-41, "What! Could you not watch with Me one hour? Watch and pray, lest you enter into temptation. The spirit indeed is willing, but the flesh is weak." Here, Christ was calling his disciples to a life of discipline and effective prayer. Years later, after Jesus had ascended into heaven, we see the power of disciplined prayer in the lives of Paul and Silas. When they were beaten and imprisoned, their resolve was not broken. At midnight, they continued in prayer, singing hymns and praising God. How could this be? Until a person has learned the value of discipline, they cannot offer sustained and effective prayer.

Our generation must return to the call of effective prayer; a prayer that focuses on Christ and divine revelation. It is a prayer whose purpose and mission are to lay hold of the Lord's assignment and perform it with such a high level of discipline and consistency that it confounds the world. The joy of Paul and Silas in the midst of their trials was historic and life-changing. Centuries later, Christians have emulated their courage and devotion, praying prayers that have changed the course of human history. Some have paid the ultimate price for their devotion to Christ; death for the sake of the gospel.

As I exhort you to a life of disciplined prayer, I encourage you to stand firm for the Kingdom of God, even in the face of persecution or threats of death. God knows how to deliver the righteous from every trouble. My prayer is that as you stand in prayer and on the Word of God, your prayer life will demonstrate your high level of devotion and commitment to Christ.

Nothing in this world matters more than being in union with Christ. No riches can surpass the peace that comes from knowing Him and spending time in prayer with Him. Prayer is everything, and effective prayer is a necessity for every living Christian. Unfortunately, in the 21st century, the fire and burden of prayer are slowly fading, producing a generation of lukewarm Christians. This has led to a lukewarm church; one that is neither hot nor cold. This is a tragedy of great proportion, as the church has allowed the devil to weaken both corporate prayer meetings and the personal prayer lives of believers. Many prayer gatherings have become mere rituals or are filled with the emotions of human needs, resembling a shopping list rather than a sincere conversation between humanity and the Divine.

Prayer should bring radical change to the individual believer, the church, and the community. Yet, many Christians pray without representation, transformation, conversion, raw, sour or genuine spiritual rebirth, as though they are not born again. The type of gospel being preached in many churches today is a material-centered gospel; one that does not focus on sin, repentance, or the need for a believer to be transformed and bear fruit. Any believer who lacks a deep connection with the Holy Spirit and is not filled with the fruit of the Spirit cannot produce effective, dynamic, and disciplined prayer.

We have witnessed Christians hopping from church to church, seeking teachers "who will tell them what their itching ears want to hear" (2 Tim. 4.3). A praying Christian must be the light of the world and the salt of the earth. Yet, we live in a generation where many Christians have lost their saltiness, and Christianity has become more about empty confessions and affirmations than true transformation. To revive Christian life and awaken the church, prayer must be restored to its central place.

It must be Christ-centered prayer, filled with the Word of God, and fueled by real faith and Christian beliefs I believe that God is awakening the church to the Spirit of prayer and that, by the turn of the 21st century, we will witness remarkable awakenings. As you read this book, make a resolution to reignite your prayer life and commit yourself to transforming your local assembly through prayer. Be the change you want to see in the church's prayer life. Make a call to effective prayer for this generation, the primacy of your Christian life and service to the Kingdom of God.

www.ingramcontent.com/pod-product-compliance
Lightning Source LLC
Chambersburg PA
CBHW041216070526
44583CB00001B/9